Tao In The Art Of Rowing

An Alpha To Zen Of Crew

Ian D. Cox MA, MD

".... a circular movement of absolutely identical series is thus demonstrated: the world as a circular movement that has already repeated itself infinitely often and plays its game ad infinitum."
Friedrich Nietzsche (The Will To Power).[1]

For information contact: rowingtao2@gmail.com

ISBN-13: 978-1511632362

Grateful acknowledgement for permission to reproduce
brain wave traces at page 43 is made to Hugo Gamboa
(Wikimedia Commons).

Cover Illustration
TAO^2 graphic: a rotated Taojitu symbol overlaid with the
profile of a rowing blade.

Table of Contents A

* See Appendices for additional tables of contents illustrating the
inter-relations of sections in the text.

Preface

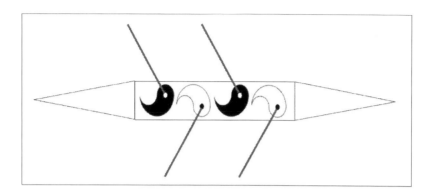

Learning to row is generally a reductive process which involves breaking the stroke down into its component parts before putting these back together as a cyclical sequence of connected actions.* However, subsequent technical progression demands a more fluid understanding of the unity of the rowing cycle. As the ultimate representation of unity, or non-duality, the Taojitu symbol seems an ideal way to represent and conceptualize this holistic view. The central Taoist principle of balance goes far deeper than the obvious bowside versus strokeside interaction in rowing, and manifests at all levels of the sport from the fine technical details of each stroke to the wider perspectives of its history and mythology. That having been said, this book is not a comprehensive account of Taoist philosophy or a detailed technical manual of rowing. The primary objective is simply to explore how the ideography and metaphysical principles of Eastern and

Western philosophy can illuminate the sport of rowing. It imagines what the great thinkers of both traditions might have shouted to us from the river bank.

---

*The text assumes readers are already familiar with the basic sequence of actions in the rowing cycle. For further information, excellent video coaching materials on basic technique and common technical faults are freely available at various internet sites including http://www.concept2.com.

Introduction

There is no escape from the repetitive nature and sometimes brutal physicality of rowing as a sport. Even so, a robotic philosophy which encourages rowers to become unthinking, boat moving machines ignores the important emotional and existential dimensions of the rowing experience. In this respect, it is essential to recognize how rowing reflects the nature of our individual consciousness as well as our collective consciousness as human beings. The rowing cycle can be seen as a microcosm of Friedrich Nietzsche's doctrine of the eternal recurrence, the central theme in the film Groundhog Day.[2,3] We repeat the same actions over and over again, seeking perfection and learning new lessons as we do. The ideal form of rowing is the elusive goal we seek and, in this quest, we are our own most important coach.* Therefore, rowing must involve both brain work and body work on and off the river. To misquote Descartes, it is the sum of the cogito and the ergo.

* Steve Fairbairn, the legendary early 20th century rowing coach, was once described as the "Socrates of the towpath", possibly as a reference to his desire to challenge orthodoxy.[4] It could be said that his belief in the existence of an innate, "ideal form" of rowing also approximated to the metaphysics of Plato. However, his rhetoric against rowers adopting a slave mentality to their coaches resonates most strongly with Friedrich Nietzsche's "will to power" philosophy.[1] As with Nietzsche, Fairbairn believed that we are each responsible for our own journey to enlightenment and, in this process, emphasized the need to avoid rigid thinking as much as rigid body movements.

A. Automaticity: Zombie Rowing

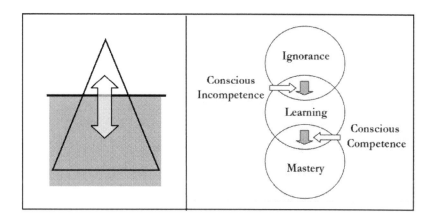

When learning any new skill, like riding a bicycle or driving a car, the initial phase involves intense concentration on every action. However, the conscious mind has limited capacity and is only the tip of the iceberg in terms of the total information processing in our brains.[5] Delegation of "routine" tasks to the subconscious is essential to allow the conscious mind to focus on critical decision making functions. Therefore, as repeated movements become familiar, they become incorporated into sub-conscious motor programs. In this way, learning progresses from conscious competence to the full mastery of unconscious competence. Such short circuiting of the conscious mind not only relieves it of unnecessary tasks but also creates additional advantages in terms of streamlining and speeding up motor functions.

The repetitive nature of rowing makes it ideally suited to this type of sub-conscious motor programming.* Once established, such programming means that the rower no longer needs to concentrate on the basic mechanics of the rowing cycle which becomes a repeated sequence of semi-automatic reflex actions. The downside of this hard wiring process is that it becomes progressively more difficult to correct established technical faults. However, unlocking the frozen subconscious programme can be achieved by downloading a new metaphor (a software patch) to refocus the conscious mind.[4] As Ludwig Wittgenstein suggested, reframing the issue can "show the fly the way out of the bottle".[6]

---

* Steve Fairbairn subscribed to a similar model of the mind characterized by: i) the objective, conscious mind responsible for "reasoning and directing"; and ii) the subjective, unconscious mind which "regulates the movements of the body".[4] Fairbairn believed that the unconscious mind, left to its own devices, was "fully competent to work the body instinctively in the best natural manner". This categorization refers primarily to the issue of objective consciousness of self during an activity rather than undivided subjective focus on the activity itself. A similar discrimination has been described in other sports and is linked to the experience of flow as discussed later.[7]

B. Balance: The Unity of Opposites

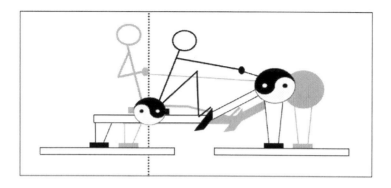

All rowers appreciate the critical importance of balance. Poor balance is the curse of the novice and good balance the joy of the skilled rower and crew. Balance is also the central theme of Taoist metaphysics, as represented by the Taojitu symbol.[8] The cyclical symmetry of the Tao is understood to reflect the balance that exists between the opposing principles of Yin and Yang in nature. The cyclical rise and fall of these opposing forces creates the ebb and flow of reality, such as day and night, or summer and winter.

The ideal form of rowing possesses a similar cyclical symmetry which can be appreciated by observing a rower on a dynamic ergometer.[9] The powerful forces generated by the rower's body are finely balanced in space and time. The extensor muscles in the legs are opposed and balanced by the flexor muscles in the arms. Consequently, with correct technique, the seat should remain virtually stationary on the slide.* As Fairbairn says, "The jerky stopping hand will catch the eye much more than the evenly moving one. Producing this to infinity a perfect oarsman's movements would be invisible."[4] The "endless chain of movement" creates stillness - this is the Tao of rowing.

---

* The sport of archery has also been used to explain the unity of opposites.[10] One arm is extended to support the bow and the other is flexed to pull the bowstring back whilst the archer's body is held in perfect stillness ready to release the arrow. Again, the balance of opposing forces simultaneously creates energy and stillness.

C. Symmetry: Cyclical Reflection

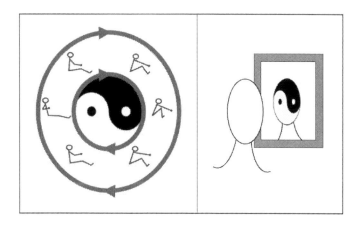

The teachings of the ancient Greek philosopher Heraclitus mirror Taoist philosophy in many important respects.[11] Heraclitus taught that all things come into being by conflict of opposites, and the sum of things flows like a stream. He also taught that the way up and the way down are one and the same. As with the Tao, this saying is understood to mean that opposing principles in the Universe come together to produce a unified whole.

Modern orthodox rowing technique also possesses a natural, cyclical symmetry like the Taojitu. The recovery phase (arms, body, legs) is performed by reversing the drive sequence (legs, body, arms).[12] In this sense, both the Tao and the rowing cycle can be conceptualized as a reflecting standing wave function. As Heraclitus might say, the way up the slide and the way down the slide are one and the same. Or more accurately, they are a reflection of each other.*

---

* The moment when a child first properly recognizes their reflection in a mirror as an image of themselves is a key milestone in early psychological development. This moment corresponds to a critical stage in the evolution of the child's reflective consciousness. This reflective, objective awareness of the self leads to a progressive expansion and refinement of the self concept through iterative discrimination of the self from the non self.[13] The same objective self awareness is also used as the inner coach to the body during sport but can also inhibit pure subjective awareness.[4,7]

D. Flow: Non-Doing

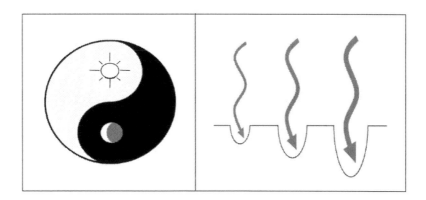

Wu Wei is a central concept in Taoist philosophy which literally means non-action or non-doing. More specifically, Wu Wei involves an attitude of non-resistance to, or harmony with, natural cycles.[8] This principle does not speak to weakness but rather a flowing form of power. Lao Tzu (the ancient Chinese sage and founder of Taoism) taught "Nothing is softer or more flexible than water, yet nothing can resist it."[8]

The Wu Wei principle does not mean that rowing can be achieved without effort. The easy way is not easy. However, this water principle does speak to a natural, fluid form of rowing which is innate within us. Steve Fairbairn quotes another coach teaching that the oar must be like an extra limb for the rower but then inverts this idea by saying that it is the rower who must become an extra part of the oar.[4] However, this idea still equates to becoming the golf club rather than the ball. As in the golfing comedy film Caddyshack, the Wu Wei principle suggests we must go further still and "be the ball"; i.e. we must become part of the natural rhythm of the river to harness the power of water.*

---

* Edward de Bono has also proposed that the way our experiences lead to changes in our brains is analogous to the way rain water erodes a rocky landscape.[14] Just as water collects into streams and rivers creating river beds and valleys, so to past experiences create established patterns of perception and movement through neuroplastic changes in the brain. This adaptive process has also been described as creating a mental "groove" for a repeated action.[7] However, with this watery model in mind, it is easy to imagine how our thinking and actions, including rowing technique, may get stuck in a rut.

E. Relativity: Einstein's Perspective

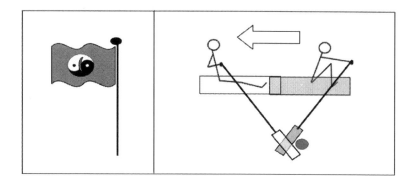

In Zen philosophy, a koan is a paradoxical story or puzzle designed to challenge conventional or orthodox thinking and, thereby, stimulate deeper reflection. One koan describes two monks watching a flag flapping in the wind. The first says "The wind is moving the flag." The second says "No, the flag is moving the wind." Overhearing the conversation, the Zen master replies "It is neither the wind nor the flag; it is your mind that is moving."*

The mechanics of rowing are more complex than the flapping flag but the same insights of relativity of motion can be adapted to the interaction between the blade and the water. The blade does not move the water and the water does not move the blade; it is the boat that moves. The water acts as a leverage point which allows the rower to move the boat past the blade. However, if the blade is not properly connected to the river at the catch, it will slip through the water preventing proper transmission of power to the boat. This is like trying to drive a car without fully engaging the clutch.

---

* Although this conclusion challenges a common sense understanding of reality, it equates well to modern phenomenological interpretations of the inter-relational foundations of our perceptions and contemporary understanding of observer effects in quantum physics.[13,15]

F. Resistance: Fluid Friction

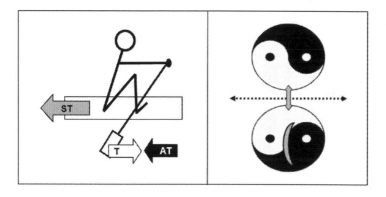

Another aspect of Wu Wei is the reversal principle which entails that nature will tend to resist our actions; a concept closely related to Newton's third law of motion (every action has an equal and opposite reaction). This natural opposition can be further understood as a dialectic process. An initial force, the thesis (T) is opposed by a natural reaction force, the antithesis (AT); the two forces then combine to create the final action, the synthesis (ST).

The mechanics of rowing can also be explained as a dialectic process. As you pull the blade towards the stern of the boat (the thesis), the force of the water naturally resists (the anti-thesis).* The water reflects the energy of the rower such that the blade and the water are locked in opposition. Ultimately, it is the boat that moves forwards (the synthesis). It is the fluid resistance force of the water opposing the force of the blade which enables the desired forward motion of the boat. This is analogous to the friction force of a car tyre on the road. If a tyre has no traction on the road then the wheels spin without moving the car. If nature did not resist the blade, it would simply slide through the water and the boat would not move.

---

* The coaching process can also be conceptualized as a dialectic process. As Arthur Eggar describes in his introduction to Fairbairn's Rowing Notes, "Moreover, the phrase usually contains an exaggeration of some notion which is applied to counteract an opposite notion which the coach seeks to eradicate, and the apparent fallacy of the exaggeration is not shown in the result when the crew arrive at the mean between the two notions."[4]

G. Connectivity: Zero Gravity

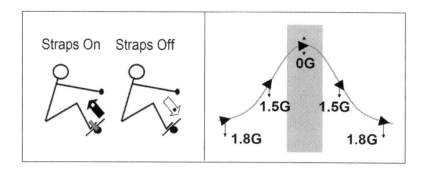

The term "bootstrapping" is derived from the phrase pulling oneself up by one's bootstraps, and is used to refer to a self-organizing process.[15,16] One example of boot-strapping is the way a child builds up their language skills using a few basic rules of grammar which govern the way words can be connected in meaningful sequence. A clear understanding of the basic principles provides the necessary starting point in a self perpetuating process of improvement.

The bootstrap principle of rowing is that, with well balanced technique, the external force of a bootstraps attaching the feet to the stretcher should be unnecessary. Understanding this principle is the basis of a natural, self-organizing rowing cycle. The interaction between the feet and the stretcher directly mediates the balanced opposition between the rower's body movement and the movement of the boat. Therefore, the force of the feet against the stretcher must be maintained throughout the drive phase. Maintaining similar balanced connection with the foot stretcher during the recovery is also essential to coordinating your movement with the run of the boat. The most difficult transition phase is at the finish. To understand this better, imagine the changes in boat reaction force at the finish as being like the moment when ground reaction force is lost when driving a car over the apex of a humpback bridge. This is also equivalent to the moment of zero gravity at the apex of a parabolic flight, as illustrated in the diagram above. The secret to maintaining connection and balance at this critical point is to row the finish fully out before rhythmically swinging the upper body weight from the hips back onto the feet. Foot pressure should then build progressively from the start of the recovery phase in preparation for the next catch.

---

* As Fairbairn said: "The stretcher is as important for rowing against as the ground is for standing on."[4] In this sense, the straps may actually encourage poor technique and this should be checked with regular "feet out" practice. This is especially true on a static ergometer where the motion of the boat is not available to assist the recovery phase. Straps on, straps off (see The Karate Kid 1984).

H. Spin: Hand Speed

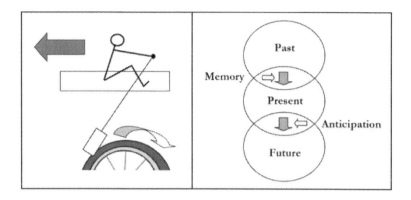

The complex interaction between the blade and the water can be further conceptualized by imagining your hand spinning an upturned bicycle wheel. If the hand is moving slowly when it first engages the wheel then the wheel must slow down to match the speed of the hand. Likewise, the final speed of the wheel at the end of the stroke is determined by the speed of the hand as it loses contact. To spin the wheel effectively, the hand must be moving forwards at equivalent speed to the wheel at first contact and then accelerate through the stroke. The faster the wheel is spinning, the more difficult this is to achieve.

A rapid pick up in blade speed at the catch and progressive acceleration of the blade is also key to an effective drive phase.[12] If the blade enters the water at a speed less than the speed of the water then the blade will act as a brake. Likewise, if the blade slows towards the end of the stroke then the final speed of the boat at the send will be reduced. Unlike a cyclist, a rower has a fixed gearing on the blade during an outing; one simply has to "pedal" faster as boat speed increases. The faster the boat is moving, the faster the river is spinning and the more critical timing becomes. Therefore, at higher speeds, the catch must become an active anticipation rather than simply a reactive process.[17] The sprinter Lynford Christie said that you have to "go on the B of the bang". Likewise, you have to go on the C of the catch to keep up with a fast moving boat.*

---

* The temporal function of human consciousness enables us not simply to react to events in the present but also to anticipate the future. In rowing terms, this predictive function can create a time dilation effect similar to that described in Einstein's Special Theory of Relativity. The experience of time passing in a rapidly moving boat can be stretched out through speed of thought and collective anticipation (synchronicity); this does not mean passively following the stroke but actively tuning in to the same rhythm.

I. Interaction: Effective Opposition

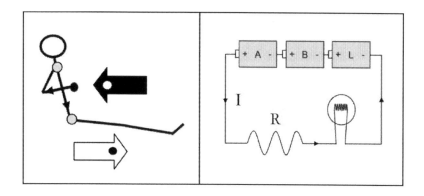

Another Zen koan is the question "What is the sound of one hand clapping?" As with all koans, there is no simple answer to this question. One possible lesson is the realization that the mind and the koan themselves have become like two hands clapping together.

The clapping principle of balanced opposition also applies to the rowing cycle. The opposition and connection between the arms and the legs through the core of the body is essential throughout the drive phase.[4] If the lower back collapses at the catch then the force of the leg drive will not be transmitted to the arms and the water.* Likewise, if the leg drive collapses before the finish is pulled up by the arms, then the arms will lose drive connection to the water and the finish will be weak. In rowing terms, this is the sound of one hand clapping.

* The rowing cycle can be compared to an electrical circuit which depends on maintaining continuity between all elements to allow the energy current (I) to flow. The diagram above illustrates the major elements of this circuit. The three batteries are the arms (A), body (B) and legs (L). The resistor (R) is the water and the brightness of the bulb is the boat speed. If the three batteries become disconnected from each other then the circuit is broken and current cannot flow to generate boat speed. Thus, maintaining integrity of the rowing circuit between all three batteries is essential throughout the drive phase.

J. Spring: The Quantum Jump

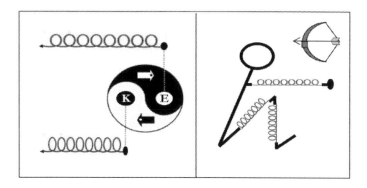

The Taojitu symbolizes the principle that natural cycles pass to one extreme before reversal occurs. Yin comes before Yang, just as the darkest hour comes before the dawn. In the same way, nature may require that you begin with the opposite to achieve your desired objective. This principle is exemplified by the sport of archery. The archer must first pull the bow string backwards in order to fire the arrow forwards.[11] Potential or elastic energy (E) is stored in the bow and the bowstring and then converted to the action or kinetic energy (K) of the arrow in flight.

The same stretch and release principle applies to the rowing cycle. Muscle power is generated by contractile proteins which cause shortening of the muscle and movement of the body. However, the muscle must be extended first to achieve the maximum effect. At the catch, elastic energy stored in the muscles of the arms and the legs is held in tension against each other, just like the two arms of the loaded bow. As with the bow, the stored energy is then released to generate kinetic energy in the boat. Creating this force of a spring under tension is critical to generating power in the drive phase, and this sequence of storing and releasing energy underpins the elastic biomechanics of the rowing cycle. During the drive phase, the legs are under maximum stretch after compression into the catch, whilst the elastic loading of the arms is maximized after the leg drive has been engaged.*

---

* Plyometric exercises ("jump training") like squat jumps are one of the mainstays of land based training for rowers. The principle of plyometrics is equivalent to "spring theory" as it focuses on moving explosively from a muscle extension to contraction (the quantum jump) in order to increase both power and speed.

K. Swing: Keeping the Momentum

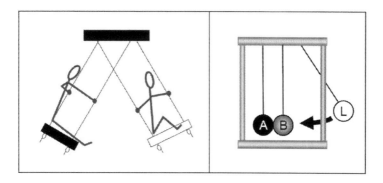

The principle of Wu Wei can also be visualized in terms of a swing. Pushing a child on a swing can be accomplished with minimum effort provided that the timing of each push is carefully coordinated with the natural cycle of the swing. Likewise, if we are swinging ourselves, changes in our body position must be carefully coordinated with the apex of the pendulum swing. Working with the natural rhythm of the swing enables maximum efficiency of effort. Pushing out of rhythm is much less effective and more uncomfortable.

The same principles apply when moving our bodies to propel a boat through the water. Maximum efficiency requires careful timing with the apex of the swing; this can only be achieved by tuning in to the rhythm of your crew, the boat and the water. Feeling the swing and timing your body movements is essential to establishing resonance in a crew and maximizing boat speed.* Spring at the catch and swing at the finish is about combining power and rhythm. With swing, the boat feels light and lively over the water; without it, the boat feels like dead weight.

---

* Newton's cradle device illustrated above can also be used to conceptualize the rowing cycle. As with Newton's cradle, conservation of momentum is the essential key to an efficient rowing cycle and this requires a dynamic synergism between the momentum of the rower's body weight and the power of the legs and arms. Newton's second law of motion states that force is equal to the product of mass and acceleration ($F = ma$). Accordingly, in order to generate force, we must accelerate our mass. As Steve Fairbairn said, "Find out how to use your weight and you will have solved the problem of how to move the boat."[4]

L. Length: The Golden Mean

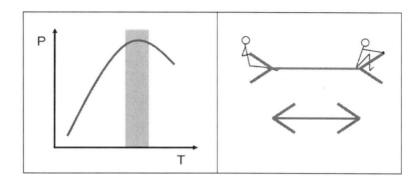

The graph above illustrates the Frank–Starling curve of cardiac function. When venous blood flow returning to the heart increases, the heart muscle becomes more stretched. The increased tension (T) in the heart muscle cells causes them to contract with greater power (P) and this helps increase cardiac output to rebalance the circulatory system. However, increasing stretch beyond a certain level becomes counterproductive to cardiac muscle function and power then starts to fall again.

The Starling principle also applies to the extension of the rower's whole body during the stroke.* Increasing stroke length generally increases power in the water. However, over-extending can also reduce power and boat speed. This analogy drawn between individual heart muscle cells and the rower's body is an example of the holographic principle.[16,18] Each of the parts in a hologram reflects the structure of the whole, as in the nested structure of a Russian doll. Likewise, the ideal rowing crew itself can be seen as a holographic structure in which the actions of the part must perfectly reflect the whole.

---

* It must also be remembered that length is not always what it seems as illustrated by the line drawing above (the Müller-Lyer Illusion). The direction of the arrows at the ends of the lines deceives the eye into thinking that the upper line is significantly longer than the one below. In fact, the two lines are of identical length. Similarly, the apparent range of a rower's body movement does not always translate into effective blade work in the water.

M. Causality: The Chain of Movement

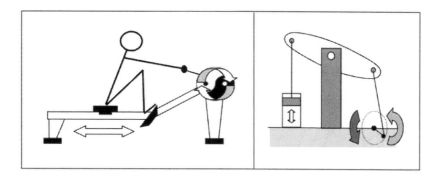

A significant contrast between Western and Eastern philosophies relates to their differing emphasis on linear and circular time and causality.[19]   Linear causal sequences have a start and a finish; an original cause and a final outcome. Circular causal sequences have no start or finish, just a continuous cycle of events like the chicken and egg.

Rowing can also be conceptualized as an interaction between linear and circular energy, as exemplified by the rowing ergometer. The linear energy we create as we move up and down the slide is converted to the circular momentum of the fly wheel. Conversely, the rowing cycle itself can be seen as a circular causal sequence of events which creates linear progress of the boat. A greater emphasis on circular energy is particularly helpful when trying to maintain body momentum at either end of the stroke. Steve Fairbairn described this circular energy as an "endless chain of movement".[4]

* As with Nietzsche's eternal recurrence,[1,2] the circular perspective is also important when trying to see the bigger picture. Linear causal sequences may just be parts of larger causal cycles, just as rivers are only part of the water cycle between land and sea.

N. Ratio: The Natural Rhythm

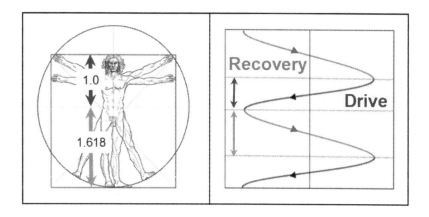

Leonardo da Vinci's "Vitruvian Man" shown above is the best known symbol of Renaissance understanding of the holographic universe. The drawing illustrates the human body perfectly inscribed within a circle and a square, the geometric symbols of heaven and earth. [20] In this way, the human body is depicted as the microcosm within the macrocosm; the part reflecting the nature of the whole. The Vitruvian Man was also understood to illustrate the "ideal" proportions of the human body characterized by the so called Golden Ratio (1:1.618) which recurs in fractal patterns throughout nature and appears to be a holographic principle of biological systems.

Just as critical sensitivity to proportion is essential to art and architectural design theory, awareness of the correct ratio between the drive and recovery phases in the rowing cycle is also fundamental to efficient technique.

As illustrated in the diagram above, the ideal rowing cycle is defined by a rapid, powerful drive and a slower, relaxed recovery.[12] Rushing the slide in the recovery phase destroys the momentum of the boat and prevents proper relaxation of the body between strokes. Conversely, allowing the run of the boat to dictate the speed and rhythm of the recovery creates the optimum, balanced rowing rhythm. At steady state, the natural drive to recovery ratio should be similar to the Golden Ratio; the ideal proportion of Vitruvian rowing.* As Claude Debussy said "Music is the space between the notes."

---

* As with the action of the heart, the rowing cycle is critically dependent on a balance between contraction and relaxation. By providing greater relaxation time in recovery, a natural Vitruvian rhythm allows greater power in the drive phase and so greater efficiency overall.

O. Rhythm: The Organic Cycle

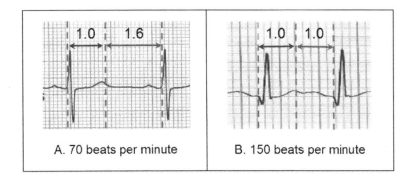

| A. 70 beats per minute | B. 150 beats per minute |

The pumping action of the heart (the cardiac cycle) consists of an active contraction phase (systole) followed by a passive relaxation phase (diastole). In the resting state with a relatively slow heart rate, the ratio of systole to diastole conforms closely to the Golden Ratio discussed in the previous section (see ECG A above).* However, at higher heart rates during exercise, the systolic to diastolic ratio is reduced to closer to 1:1 with proportionately less time for diastolic filling (ECG B). Reducing the diastolic phase below this level starts to create a reverse ratio (systole longer than diastole) which becomes counter-productive as there is insufficient time for blood flow to refill the heart chambers between beats. Consequently, the relationship between heart rate and cardiac output is similar to the Starling Curve described earlier.

The same considerations apply to the rowing cycle. As stroke rate increases, the duration of the recovery phase tends to be reduced and this limits the time available for the body to relax between strokes. However, as with the cardiac cycle, maintaining the recovery phase even at higher rates is critical to sustaining power and efficiency over longer periods. Consequently, the relationship between stroke rate and boat speed also conforms to the Starling Curve.[12] The part, again, reflects the whole.

---

*The ECG (electrocardiogram) is a recording of the electrical activity associated with heart muscle contraction during the cardiac cycle. The larger spike on the tracing (the R wave) corresponds to the start of contraction and the smaller, subsequent spike (the T wave) corresponds to the end of contraction.

P. Entrainment: Pneumatic Drill

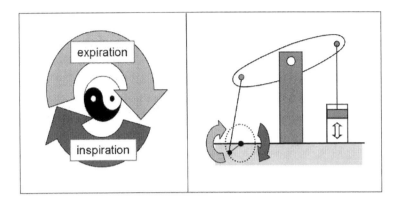

The ancient Greeks believed that life was maintained by the vital spirit or pneuma (literally meaning breath) which was produced when air drawn into the lungs was combined with blood in the heart. The equivalent Chinese word for life energy or spirit is Chi. Regulating the flow of Chi in the body is also critical for health and vitality according to the principles of Chinese medicine. This regulation can be promoted by attention to breathing rhythm and coordination of breathing with body posture, which are key principles in both meditation practices and martial arts.

The repetitive sequence of rowing actions also naturally lends itself to coordination of body movement with the respiratory rhythm. As with controlling the flow of Chi, current scientific understanding of exercise physiology also indicates that entrainment of the breathing rhythm with the phases of the rowing cycle is important to maximizing respiratory efficiency.[21]   Although the timing may vary between individuals, the descent of the diaphragm during the in breath tends to increase intra-abdominal pressure and so provides important additional support to the lower (lumbar) spine at the start of the drive phase.   This effect is equivalent to focusing your Chi in your lower abdomen during meditation or martial arts.   Therefore, optimum pneumatic drill involves catching your breath during the recovery before the catch. Breathe in to put the blade in and breathe out to pull the blade out.*

---

* A consistent relationship between body movements and respiratory effort also helps preserve the rhythm of both cycles at different stroke rates. As with the cardiac cycle, the normal breathing pattern at rest is characterized by a short, active inspiratory effort involving contraction of muscles in the chest wall and diaphragm (breathing in), followed by a longer passive expiratory phase (breathing out). However, during exercise, the expiratory phase becomes more active and relatively shorter as the breathing rate increases.

Q. Transmission: Quads versus Biceps

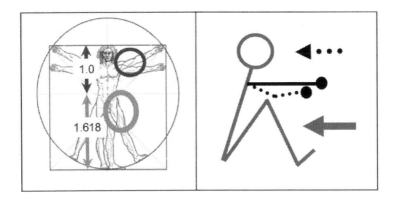

The Vitruvian Man not only illustrates the size proportions of the body but also gives a sense of the relative power of the arms and legs. Although the ratio of muscle power in the arms and legs will vary with specific training regimens, research in active individuals without specific power training suggest that the natural ratio of arm to leg power is also similar to the Golden Ratio (1:1.6).[22]

Even weight lifters are aware of the relative weakness of their arms and hold their arms straight to enable them to transmit the more powerful force from the legs at the start of a heavy lift. Likewise, the arms should be straight at the start of the drive phase in rowing to ensure that they transmit the full power of the leg-work.[12] Bent arm catches reduce the maximum power to the weakest link in the chain and so tend to prevent the full power of the leg drive being transmitted to the blade. Saving the arm draw for the final part of the drive phase is also consistent with "spring theory" as stated earlier.*

---

* Although power comes mainly from the legs, the arms move through a much wider range of motion and are responsible for generating length. Reaching out with the arms at the catch and drawing up at the finish are essential to translate the energy of the leg drive into long powerful strokes. This means getting the elbows past the knees at the catch and past the hips at the finish.

R. Resonance: Thinking of Non-Thinking

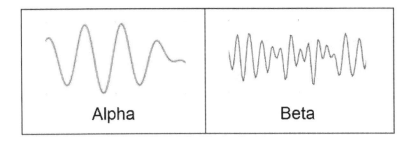

Wu Nien is the principle of empty thought or the thinking of non-thinking in Taoist philosophy.[8] In modern neurophysiological terms, this idea seems to relate to a state of deep conscious relaxation which is associated with high amplitude, low frequency Alpha brain waves as recorded on an electroencephalogram as illustrated above.* In contrast, intense concentration on mental activities and visual stimulation provoke more frenetic, low amplitude, high frequency Beta brain wave activity.

The Alpha brain state can be achieved through meditation and other relaxation techniques, including certain types of exercise. The rhythmic, repetitive nature of the rowing cycle seems ideally suited to such mental relaxation during exercise and, in this respect, is like a physical mantra.[23] The Alpha state may also be associated with the psychological state of "flow" when one is fully immersed in an activity with a feeling of energized focus, free from distraction or self consciousness.[24] Such moments of self transcendence are often described as peak experiences. Steve Fairbairn referred to this as "losing all touch with material consciousness" and becoming "in tune with the infinite".[4] Peter Mallory has termed this the "out of boat experience".[25]

---

* The EEG tracing records the summation of all the brain's electrical activity through an external recording made with electrodes attached to the surface of the scalp. The larger Alpha waves reflect a greater degree of resonance i.e. constructive interference between different in phase electrical waveforms in the brain. The smaller, more frenetic Beta wave pattern reflects more destructive interference between multiple out of phase electrical waveforms. Most rowers will also recognize the Beta boat experience.

S. Synchronicity: The Collective Alpha

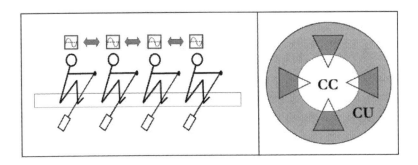

The fact that human beings are the dominant species on Earth is commonly attributed to our large brains. However, it is not just the size but the connectivity of our brains which is the secret of our success. Humans are able to transfer complex information from one brain to another through a sophisticated combination of verbal and non-verbal communication. This ability enables us to collaborate in large social groups and, with our associated technology, has now created a global human community with a collective intelligence far greater than that of any individual.

It has been argued that rowing represents the ultimate example of human collaboration in sport, and the enjoyment of working in close harmony with others is a central part of the rowing experience. The state of resonance or synchronicity* created by a crew in perfect unison may be particularly conducive to relaxation, even during intense exercise.[23] Under the right circumstances, these factors can produce a collective

Alpha experience and the sense of flow in a whole crew.[26] In the words of Fairbairn, "Rowing together is harmony, and harmony produces greater harmony."[4]

---

* The term synchronicity was first used by the psychoanalyst Carl Jung who extended Freud's model of the mind by highlighting an additional level of collective consciousness (CC) and a collective unconscious (CU).[27] In Jung's terminology, synchronicity refers to events linked indirectly by meaning rather than direct causality. Such acausal connections are understood to relate to collective beliefs and understanding rather than physical forces.

T. Tension: Meaningful Combination

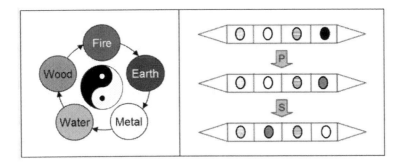

Like the Tao, Wu Xing theory proposes that the Universe is governed by cycles of creation and destruction reflecting the directional flow of energy between five elements or phases, which are wood, fire, earth, metal and water. According to traditional Chinese Medicine, it is by working in harmony with these cycles that health and success are achieved.

The blending of different elements within a rowing crew is also essential to success. Most crews contain a diverse mixture of personalities with different strengths and weaknesses.[28] Although oppositions within a crew may adversely affect the overall dynamic, they may also be a source of constructive and creative tension. This idea is similar to the principle behind medieval alchemy where different base metals were mixed in the hope of creating gold. You do not necessarily have to be like your crewmates or even have to like them.[26] However, it is essential that you row like them in order to combine effectively together.

* The crew selection process can be conceptualized in linguistic terms as the creation of meaning. Composing a sentence involves both word selection (paradigmatic; P) choices and word order (syntagmatic; S) choices. Both types of choices are critical to the final meaning. As with a sentence, sequence changes and individual substitutions in a crew may create or destroy coherence.

U. Limits: Understanding Yourself

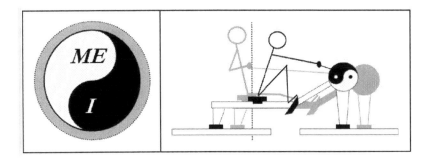

Felix Baumgartner's high altitude parachute jump from the limits of the Earth's atmosphere in 2012 must surely represent one of the most inspiring sporting moments in recent history. After years of technical and psychological struggle, Baumgartner finally made his leap of faith from an altitude of 39 kilometres, thereby redefining his own limits, as well as the limits of his sport.

As with Baumgartner, your rowing goals are created by your imagination and then your limits are defined by striving for your goals. We find out who we are in the liminal space between what we can and cannot do. That is, you must find your limits in order to realize your full potential. To paraphrase the philosophy of the hero in the film Dirty Harry, a good man or woman knows their limitations.*

* The reflective function of human consciousness entails an ability to perceive ourselves objectively (Me) in a manner separated from our immediate subjective awareness and feelings (I).[7,13] In addition, a third, synthetic position allows us to balance these two perspectives. This intrapersonal dialectic could be said to represent the essence of the Self.

V. Flux: Infinite Variety

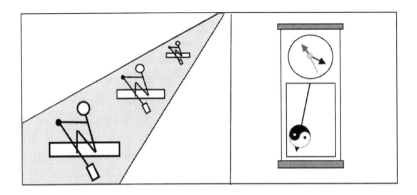

Taoist metaphysics is based on the principle that the Universe is subject to continual cycles of change as described in the Yi Ching (Books Of Changes).[8] The teachings of Heraclitus describe a similar concept of flux which he illustrated by the saying that "You cannot step into the same river twice."[11] The river appears to be a relatively constant feature in the landscape but the water in the river is continually changing, as is everything around the river, including yourself.*

Heraclitus would presumably also assert that you cannot row in the same river twice, or even row the same stroke twice. The external variables (including the weather, the state of the river, the mood of rest of the crew etc.) and internal variables (your mood, your physical condition etc.) are almost infinite. Therefore, although the repetitive aspects of the rowing cycle have been emphasized, the conditions are different each time we row and this is also reflected in the continual changes in ourselves. Our bodies are constantly repairing and recycling their component parts. Ultimately, like the ship of Theseus in Greek mythology, all the parts are replaced and only the whole maintains continuity with the past. The rower and the river are both in flux.

---

* The flux principle would seem superficially to be at odds with the idea of eternal cycles and recurrence.[2] However, Nietzsche himself suggested that Heraclitus' teachings promoted a belief in eternal recurrence.[29] As discussed previously, the river is only part of the water cycle between land and sea.

W. Collectivity: The Third World

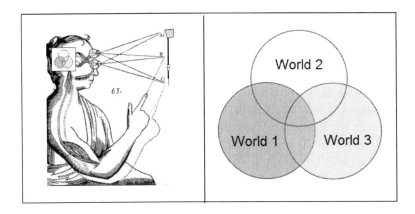

Any attempt to characterize human consciousness must take proper account of the social dimension of our minds.[27] Karl Popper recognized this in his three world model of consciousness by extending Descartes dualistic mind versus matter perspective.[30] As well as the World 1 of physical reality and World 2 of subjective awareness, Popper's model also includes World 3, the social domain of inter-subjective reality manifested in human culture and collective understanding. Physical artifacts of human consciousness (like a boat or a blade) exist at the intersection between World 1 and World 3 in this construct.*

By recognizing the critical collectivity of human consciousness, Popper's model also serves as a useful framework for strategic awareness in the boat. Being alert to changes in the physical environment, your own internal state and your human environment (crew mates and the opposition) is the key. As Sun Tzu wrote, "Know the enemy, know yourself; your victory will never be endangered. Know the ground, know the weather; your victory will then be total."[31]

---

* Popper's social domain of World 3 also corresponds to Carl Jung's view of collective consciousness in human social groups. However, Jungian theory also proposes a collective unconscious which contains specific forms or "archetypes" which reflect recurring themes in human culture and mythology. Likewise, a shared local or global rowing history and mythology combined with a common understanding of the rowing cycle also provides the basis for deep synchronicity in a crew. [32]

X. Synergism: Multiplication Of Effort

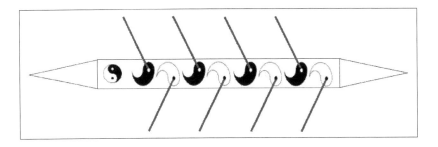

There is little doubt that the course of human history has hinged on the ability of different human groups to collaborate successfully. The rise and fall of empires has largely been determined by the ability to create and maintain cohesion of large groups through commitment to a common cause. The key is harnessing the energy of many individuals into a collective endeavour which is greater than themselves. Such human collaboration obeys the law of multiplication rather than simple addition. The synergism of the group means that the function of the whole is greater than the sum of the parts.*

Squad selection is a microcosm of the competitive human macrocosm. We compete to be in a crew and compete within a crew. However, ultimate success depends on our ability to collaborate and compete as a crew. Furthermore, once established in a crew, the commitment to the common team cause is often a more powerful force than individual motivation. Competitive collaboration is the paradoxical winning formula and this means connecting with each other as well as connecting with the river.

---

* The eight is the fastest boat on the river but also the most challenging to coach in terms of achieving and maintaining group coherence. Poor coordination of effort rather than a lack of muscle power is often the main limiting factor in respect to the maximizing boat speed. Establishing Alpha resonance through synchronicity ensures each member of the crew is working with and not against the whole.

Y. Competition: Yin and Yang

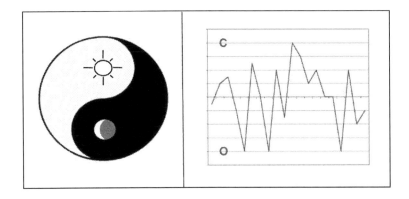

The experiences of winning and losing in competition can feel like day and night. Hugh Laurie's Retrospective Theory further proposes that winning at rowing is better than winning at any other sport because you are facing backwards and, therefore, able to enjoy the sight of your opponents losing.[33]   Likewise, losing is made worse because the opposition is out of sight. However, losing a close side by side finish may be the worst experience of all. A rower may obsess for months or years about the small factors which contributed to a narrow defeat, whereas it may be easier to draw a line under an outcome which was beyond reasonable doubt.

Although the will to win is a critical element in success, embracing the Tao of rowing also means recognizing the larger cycle of events.* Each victory or defeat is a new beginning. The meaning of rowing lies neither in the winning nor the losing but in the striving that precedes competition and of which competition is comprised. The secret to success often lies in prior failures and a willingness to accept defeat as the necessary prerequisite of victory. The Yin contains the seed of the Yang.

---

* The graph above represents the fluctuating fortunes of Oxford and Cambridge in the University Boat Race since the first race in 1829. Like the Tao, these cycles of victory and defeat represent the ebb and flow of opposing trends in the two crews over the decades.[34] As of 2015, Cambridge have won 81 times and Oxford have won 79 times. The balance of the Universe is almost restored.

Z. Narrative: Zenith to Nadir

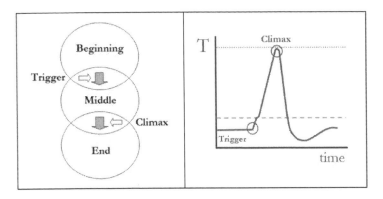

Narrative is the most sophisticated form of language and is fundamental to human consciousness and communication.[35]   Describing narrative structure, Aristotle said that a whole is what has a beginning, middle and an end. This classical three part structure was subsequently elaborated in Gustav Freytag's pyramid model which describes successive stages of rising and falling tension (T). This narrative sequence has an initial trigger which leads through a chain of causally related events to a climactic ending before tension once again subsides to baseline levels, as illustrated by the graph above.*

The rowing cycle also has a natural narrative structure involving a series of causally related events. Composing an effective stroke requires the same pattern of rising tension as composing an emotive story. In this sense, the catch is the trigger event with tension then rising throughout the drive phase. One action leads to the next in a self-organizing sequence culminating in the climactic finish. However, like the Tao, each story is just a part of a much larger cycle of events.[36] The end of one stroke is just the beginning of the next.

---

* Freytag's pyramid model of narrative structure is illustrated above in the form of an action potential, the electrical signal generated by a single nerve cell. This action potential format illustrates a holographic correspondence between the most basic and the most sophisticated aspects of brain function.[15,18]

Last Words

Rowing is like Groundhog Day; its meaning lies in passing through the same events over and over again, continually striving for perfection. As Aristotle taught, "We are what we repeatedly do; excellence, then, is not an act, but a habit." Edward Whymper, a pioneer of Alpine moutaineering similarly advised prospective mountaineers to "look well to each step". Likewise, Steve Fairbairn's rowing philosophy might be stated as look well to every stroke. Or, as he said, "The race is only an illustration of how you rowed each stroke in practice, and so the next stroke is really the race."[4] This emphasis on the significance of every action speaks again to a holographic perspective. It also suggests a preconception of chaos theory in which each stroke is like the flap of a butterfly's wings which may eventually lead to a hurricane. However, like the butterfly, the essence of the ideal rowing technique is its dynamic, temporal nature and this cannot be captured in words alone.* The Tao that can be spoken is not the eternal

Tao and the stroke that can be rowed is not the ideal form of rowing. To give Fairbairn the last words, "One can never really row; one can only illustrate in a boat what one thinks rowing is."[4]

Appendix 1: Table of Contents B

	Introduction	Last Words	
	Introduction	Last Words	
A	Automaticity	Resonance	R
B	Balance	Symmetry	C
D	Flow	Flux	V
E	Relativity	Spin	H
F	Resistance	Interaction	I
G	Connectivity	Collectivity	W
J	Spring	Swing	K
L	Length	Limits	U
M	Causality	Synchronicity	S
N	Ratio	Transmission	Q
O	Rhythm	Entrainment	P
T	Tension	Narrative	Z
X	Synergism	Competition	Y

This table illustrates the symmetries and balanced opposition between related elements in the text.

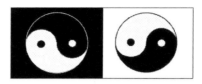

Appendix 2: Table of Contents C

Rower
A. Automaticity
B. Balance
C. Symmetry
N. Ratio
O. Rhythm
P. Entrainment
U. Limits
Z. Narrative

↑

Finish	Crew	Catch
	R. Resonance	
G. Connectivity	S. Synchronicity	H. Spin
I. Interaction	T. Tension	J. Spring
K. Swing	W. Collectivity	L. Length
M. Causality	X. Synergism	Q. Transmission
	Y. Competition	

↓

River
D. Flow
E. Relativity
F. Resistance
V. Flux

The cardinal elements of this table relate to the balanced opposition between the rower and river, and the catch and the finish. The central elements relate to team dynamics and the link between the whole and the part. See also the related ideographic representation in Appendix 3.

Appendix 3: Mandala*

---

* A mandala is an ideographic device used in both Eastern and Western philosophy[20,27] which utilizes geometric forms to symbolize a unified view of reality. The mandala above symbolizes the essential principles of rowing. The cardinal elements represent the energy of the arms and legs reflected at the catch and finish and the energy of the rower's body reflected in the river. The rotational symmetry of the mandala represents the rotational symmetry of the rowing cycle and the central element represents the holographic principle in rowing.

References

[1] Will To Power: The Philosophy Of Friedrich Nietzsche.
RC Solomon, & KM Higgins. Chantilly, VA: Teaching Co., 1999.

[2] Eternal Recurrence by Matt McDonald.
http://myweb.lmu.edu/tshanahan/Nietzsche-Eternal_Recurrence.html

[3] The Motivated Mind.
Raj Persaud. London: Bantam Books, 2005.

[4] On Rowing – The Complete Series.
Steve Fairbairn, with Peter Mallory. https://www.rowperfect.co.uk,
2014.

[5] The Wayward Mind: An Intimate History of the Unconscious.
Guy Claxton. London: Abacus 2006.

[6] Philosophical Investigations, 4th edition.
Ludwig Wittgenstein, P.M.S. Hacker and Joachim Schulte (eds. and
trans.). Oxford: Wiley-Blackwell, 2009.

[7] The Inner Game Of Tennis.
W. Timothy Gallwey. London: Pan Macmillan, 1986.

[8] Tao: The Watercourse Way.
Alan Watts, with Al Chung-Liang Huang. New York: Pantheon
/Random House, 1975.

[9] Rowing On Slides
http://www.concept2.com/indoor-rowers/training/technique-
videos/using-slides

[10] Zen in the Art of Archery.
Eugen Herrigel. New York: Pantheon Books, 1953.

[11] The Art and Thought of Heraclitus.
Edited by Charles H. Kahn. Cambridge University Press, 1979.

[12] Steven Redgrave's Complete Book of Rowing.
Steven Redgrave. London: Partridge Press, 1995.

[13] The Interpreted World: An Introduction To Phenomenological

Psychology (2nd Edition).
Ernesto Spinelli. London: Sage Publications, 2005.

[14] Water Logic.
Edward de Bono. London: Penguin Books, 1994.

[15] The Tao of Physics.
Fritjof Capra. Berkeley, California: Shambhala Publications, 1975.

[16] The Turning Point.
Fritjof Capra. New York: Simon & Schuster, 1982.

[17] Bounce: The Myth of Talent and the Power of Practice.
Matthew Syed. New York: Harper Collins, 2010.

[18] The Holographic Universe.
Michael Talbot. London: HarperCollins, 1996.

[19] The Nature Of Time.
GJ Whitrow. New York: Holt, Rinehart & Winston Inc., 1973.

[20] Sacred Architecture.
AT Mann. Rockport: Element Inc., 1993.

[21] Assessment of the timing of respiration during rowing and its relationship to spinal kinematics. Bateman *et al.*. Biology of Sport 2006; Vol. 23 No4. biolsport.com/fulltxt.php?ICID=890800

[22] Anaerobic power of the arms and legs of young and older men. Marsh *et al.*. Experimental Physiology 1999;84(3):589-97. http://www.ncbi.nlm.nih.gov/pubmed/10362857

[23] Hanlan's Spirit: Training For Flow
Jimmy Joy. New York: The Joy of Sculling, 2013.

[24] Flow: The Psychology of Optimal Experience
Mihaly Csikszentmihalyi. New York: Harper Collins 1990.

[25] An Out-of-Boat Experience.
Peter Mallory. The San Diego Writers' Monthly Press, 2002.

[26] Zen and the elite art of rowing. Peter Popham.
http://www.independent.co.uk/life-style/zen-and-the-elite-art-of-rowing-1275674.html

[27] Jung To Live By.
Eugene Pascal. New York: Warner Books Inc., 1992.

[28] Four Men in a Boat.
Tim Foster, Rory Ross. London: Weidenfeld & Nicolson, 2004.

[29] Of the Bow and the Lyre: Nietzsche's Theory of Eternal Recurrence.
Alan Green. ProQuest, UMI Dissertation Publishing, 2011.

[30] Meditations on First Philosophy.
Rene Descartes (ed. John Cottingham). Cambridge University Press, 1996.

[31] Sun Tzu's The Art of War.
Sun Tzu. El Paso: Norte, 2005.

[32] The Story Of World Rowing.
Christopher Dodd. London: Stanley Paul & Co., 1992.

[33] Hugh Laurie explains motivation in rowing.
https://www.youtube.com/watch?v=cHq0kYgD1ZI

[34] Boat Race - The Oxford Revival.
Daniel Topolski. London: Willow Books, 1985.

[35] Foundations of Interactive Narrative: A Theory Review.
Zach Tomaszewski.
http://www2.hawaii.edu/~ztomasze/ics699/intnarr.html

[36] A Lifetime In A Race.
Matthew Pinsent. London: Ebury Press, 2004.

Printed in Great Britain
by Amazon